FINGER WORKS

All letters can be made with a COMBINATION of the following BASIC STROKES:

Look at the following groups of letters with your child. Have him or her TRACE the strokes with a FINGER.

VERTICAL line begins at the TOP

HORIZONTAL line begins at the LEFT

SLANTED line begins at the top

CIRCLES begin at 2:00 o'clock and go up and around

REVERSE CIRCLE

ABCDEFGHIJKLMN
OPQRST UVWXYZ
abcdef ghijklmn
opqrst uvwxyz

1. Trace the basic strokes with your pencil.

2. Draw a line from the basic stroke to the letter that it matches.

Talk together about which strokes make up each letter.

3

ADVENTURE ROAD: Find your way along the road to the castle. Keep your pencil on the page. Try to stay on the road. Connect all the horseshoes.

Left

Right

Curve

Slant

AaBbCcDdEeFfGgHhIiJjKkLlMmNnOoPpQqRrSsTtUuVvWwXxYyZz

BASIC STROKES FOR LETTER COMBINATIONS

BEFORE WRITING

Before each lesson, review the letter previously learned

Before each lesson, assist your child in answering the following questions.

1. What is the name of each letter?
2. How many spaces does the letter use?
3. How many strokes make up the letter?
4. Where does each stroke start and stop?

STARTING TO PRINT

1. Trace the letter with your pencil as well as you can.
2. Remember to lift your pencil after each stroke.
3. Try to copy the same letter in the empty space.

*IT'S OK TO MAKE A MISTAKE

BEGIN: Trace the stroke, following the arrows. Using the color pencil. Write the stroke in the empty space. Wipe surface clean with a damp cloth. Have patience.

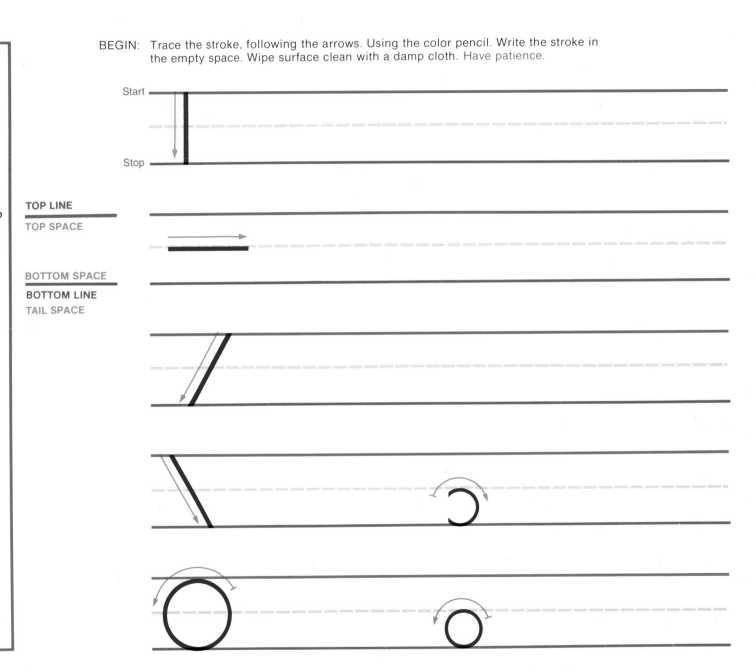

Aa Bb Cc Dd Ee Ff Gg Hh Ii Jj Kk Ll Mm Nn Oo Pp Qq Rr Ss Tt Uu Vv Ww Xx Yy Zz

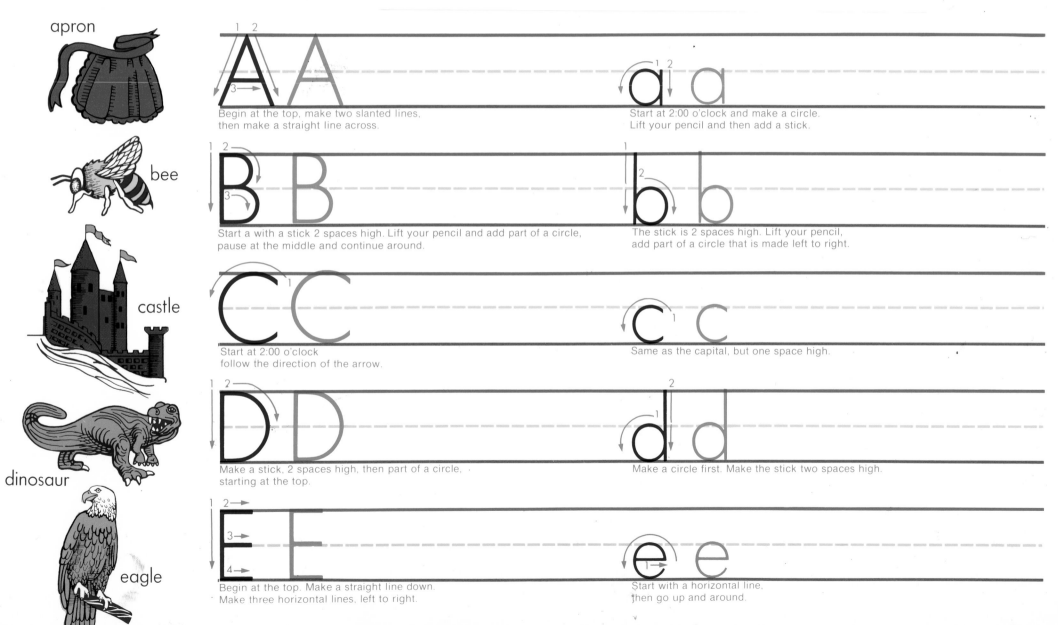

apron

bee

castle

dinosaur

eagle

A A
Begin at the top, make two slanted lines,
then make a straight line across.

a a
Start at 2:00 o'clock and make a circle.
Lift your pencil and then add a stick.

B B
Start a with a stick 2 spaces high. Lift your pencil and add part of a circle,
pause at the middle and continue around.

b b
The stick is 2 spaces high. Lift your pencil,
add part of a circle that is made left to right.

C C
Start at 2:00 o'clock
follow the direction of the arrow.

c c
Same as the capital, but one space high.

D D
Make a stick, 2 spaces high, then part of a circle,
starting at the top.

d d
Make a circle first. Make the stick two spaces high.

E E
Begin at the top. Make a straight line down.
Make three horizontal lines, left to right.

e e
Start with a horizontal line,
then go up and around.

AaBbCcDdEeFfGgHhIiJjKkLlMmNnOoPpQqRrSsTtUuVvWwXxYyZz

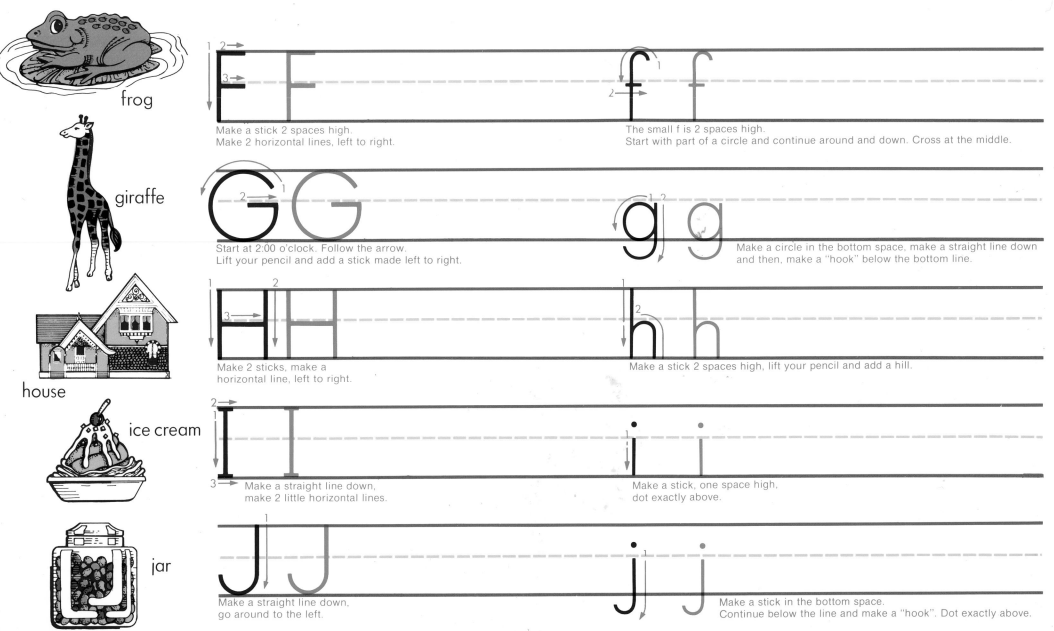

frog

giraffe

house

ice cream

jar

F
Make a stick 2 spaces high.
Make 2 horizontal lines, left to right.

f
The small f is 2 spaces high.
Start with part of a circle and continue around and down. Cross at the middle.

G
Start at 2:00 o'clock. Follow the arrow.
Lift your pencil and add a stick made left to right.

g
Make a circle in the bottom space, make a straight line down and then, make a "hook" below the bottom line.

H
Make 2 sticks, make a
horizontal line, left to right.

h
Make a stick 2 spaces high, lift your pencil and add a hill.

I
Make a straight line down,
make 2 little horizontal lines.

i
Make a stick, one space high,
dot exactly above.

J
Make a straight line down,
go around to the left.

j
Make a stick in the bottom space.
Continue below the line and make a "hook". Dot exactly above.

11

Aa Bb Cc Dd Ee Ff Gg Hh Ii Jj Kk Ll Mm Nn Oo Pp Qq Rr Ss Tt Uu Vv Ww Xx Yy Zz

NOTA DE PEDIDO DE LAPICES

APRENDIENDO A ESCRIBIR LAS LETRAS (Bilingüe)

U.S.A. $1.25 cada lápiz.
Canada & Mexico — Giro Postal Internacional $1.25
Otros Países — Giro Postal Internacional $1.50

CANTIDAD		TOTAL $
AZUL	VERDE	
ROJO	MARRON	

Residentes de N.Y. añadir impuesto sobre ventas

(Dólares Americanos) TOTAL ADJUNTO _____ $ _____

NOMBRE _____

DIRECCION _____

CIUDAD _____

ESTADO _____ CODIGO POSTAL _____

PAIS _____

Haga el giro postal a:
PEN NOTES INC.
134 West Side Ave. • Freeport, New York 11520-5499 • U.S.A.

PENCIL ORDER FORM

LEARNING TO PRINT	**LEARN HANDWRITING**
LEARNING TO TELL TIME	**LEARN TO WRITE NUMBERS**

U.S.A. $1.25 each pencil.
Canada & Mexico International Postal Money Order **$1.25 each**
All Other Countries — International Postal Money Order **$1.50 each**

QUANTITY		TOTAL $
BLUE	GREEN	
RED	BROWN	

N.Y.S. Residents add sales tax

(U.S. Dollars) AMOUNT ENCLOSED _____ $ _____

NAME _____

ADDRESS _____

CITY _____

STATE _____ ZIP _____

COUNTRY _____

Make check or money order payable to: **PEN NOTES INC.**
134 West Side Ave. • Freeport, New York 11520-5499 • U.S.A.

PENCIL ORDER FORM

LEARNING TO PRINT	**LEARN HANDWRITING**
LEARNING TO TELL TIME	**LEARN TO WRITE NUMBERS**

U.S.A. $1.25 each pencil.
Canada & Mexico International Postal Money Order **$1.25 each**
All Other Countries — International Postal Money Order **$1.50 each**

QUANTITY		TOTAL $
BLUE	GREEN	
RED	BROWN	

N.Y.S. Residents add sales tax

(U.S. Dollars) AMOUNT ENCLOSED _____ $ _____

NAME _____

ADDRESS _____

CITY _____

STATE _____ ZIP _____

COUNTRY _____

Make check or money order payable to: **PEN NOTES INC.**
134 West Side Ave. • Freeport, New York 11520-5499 • U.S.A.

PENCIL ORDER FORM

LEARNING TO PRINT	**LEARN HANDWRITING**
LEARNING TO TELL TIME	**LEARN TO WRITE NUMBERS**

U.S.A. $1.25 each pencil.
Canada & Mexico International Postal Money Order **$1.25 each**
All Other Countries — International Postal Money Order **$1.50 each**

QUANTITY		TOTAL $
BLUE	GREEN	
RED	BROWN	

N.Y.S. Residents add sales tax

(U.S. Dollars) AMOUNT ENCLOSED _____ $ _____

NAME _____

ADDRESS _____

CITY _____

STATE _____ ZIP _____

COUNTRY _____

Make check or money order payable to: **PEN NOTES INC.**
134 West Side Ave. • Freeport, New York 11520-5499 • U.S.A.

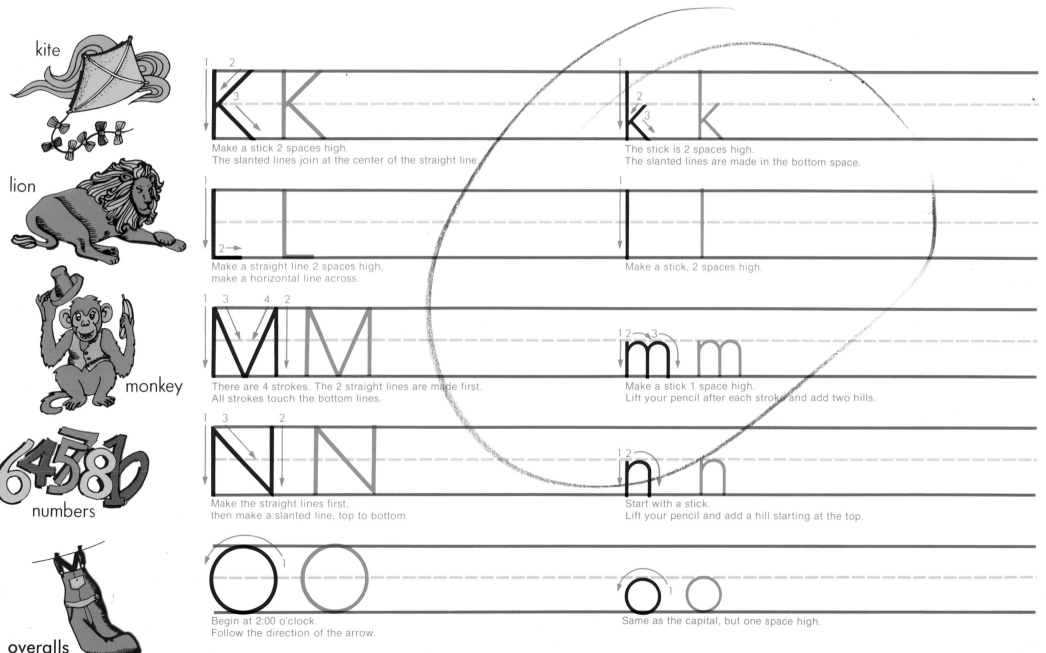

kite

lion

monkey

numbers

overalls

K Make a stick 2 spaces high.
The slanted lines join at the center of the straight line.

k The stick is 2 spaces high.
The slanted lines are made in the bottom space.

L Make a straight line 2 spaces high,
make a horizontal line across.

l Make a stick, 2 spaces high.

M There are 4 strokes. The 2 straight lines are made first.
All strokes touch the bottom lines.

m Make a stick 1 space high.
Lift your pencil after each stroke and add two hills.

N Make the straight lines first,
then make a slanted line, top to bottom.

n Start with a stick.
Lift your pencil and add a hill starting at the top.

O Begin at 2:00 o'clock.
Follow the direction of the arrow.

o Same as the capital, but one space high.

13

Aa Bb Cc Dd Ee Ff Gg Hh Ii Jj Kk Ll Mm Nn Oo Pp Qq Rr Ss Tt Uu Vv Ww Xx Yy Zz

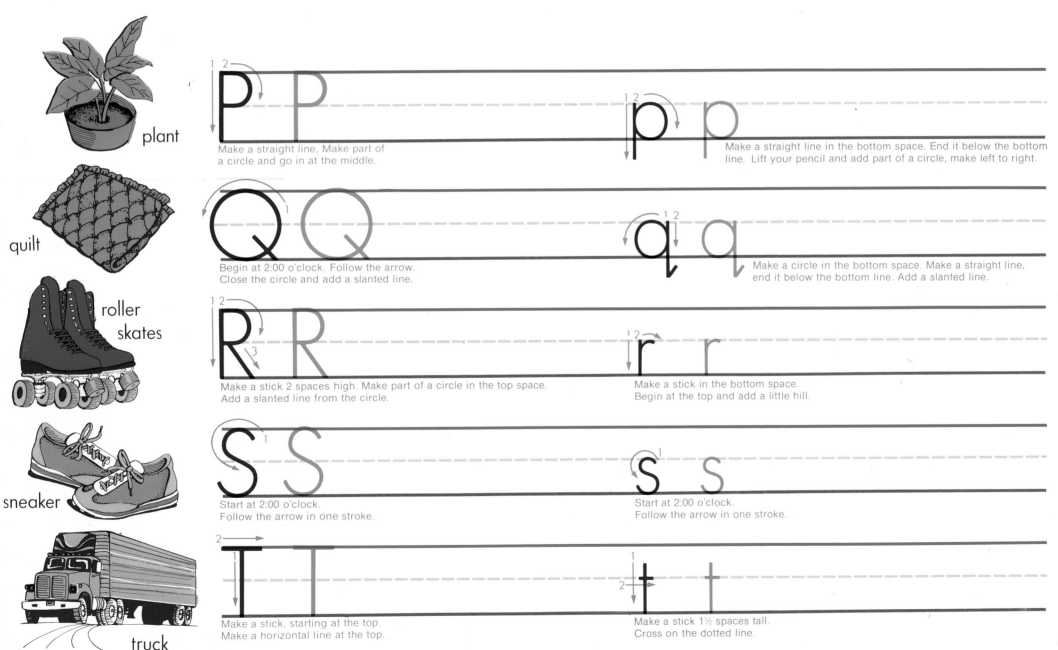

plant

P
Make a straight line, Make part of
a circle and go in at the middle.

p
Make a straight line in the bottom space. End it below the bottom
line. Lift your pencil and add part of a circle, make left to right.

quilt

Q
Begin at 2:00 o'clock. Follow the arrow.
Close the circle and add a slanted line.

q
Make a circle in the bottom space. Make a straight line,
end it below the bottom line. Add a slanted line.

roller
skates

R
Make a stick 2 spaces high. Make part of a circle in the top space.
Add a slanted line from the circle.

r
Make a stick in the bottom space.
Begin at the top and add a little hill.

S
Start at 2:00 o'clock.
Follow the arrow in one stroke.

sneaker

s
Start at 2:00 o'clock.
Follow the arrow in one stroke.

T
Make a stick, starting at the top.
Make a horizontal line at the top.

t
Make a stick 1½ spaces tall.
Cross on the dotted line.

truck

Aa Bb Cc Dd Ee Ff Gg Hh Ii Jj Kk Ll Mm Nn Oo Pp Qq Rr Ss Tt Uu Vv Ww Xx Yy Zz

To practice here, turn the book around and flip the plastic page.

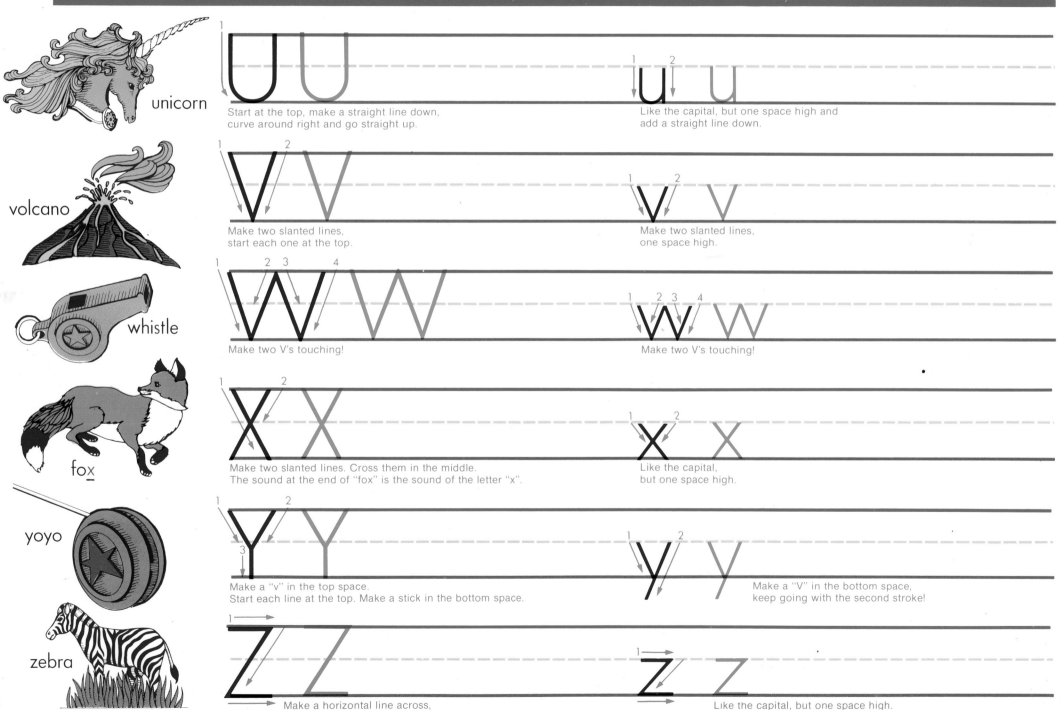

unicorn

Start at the top, make a straight line down,
curve around right and go straight up.

Like the capital, but one space high and
add a straight line down.

volcano

Make two slanted lines,
start each one at the top.

Make two slanted lines,
one space high.

whistle

Make two V's touching!

Make two V's touching!

fox

Make two slanted lines. Cross them in the middle.
The sound at the end of "fox" is the sound of the letter "x".

Like the capital,
but one space high.

yoyo

Make a "v" in the top space.
Start each line at the top. Make a stick in the bottom space.

Make a "V" in the bottom space,
keep going with the second stroke!

zebra

Make a horizontal line across,
a slanted line down to the left, and another line across.

Like the capital, but one space high.

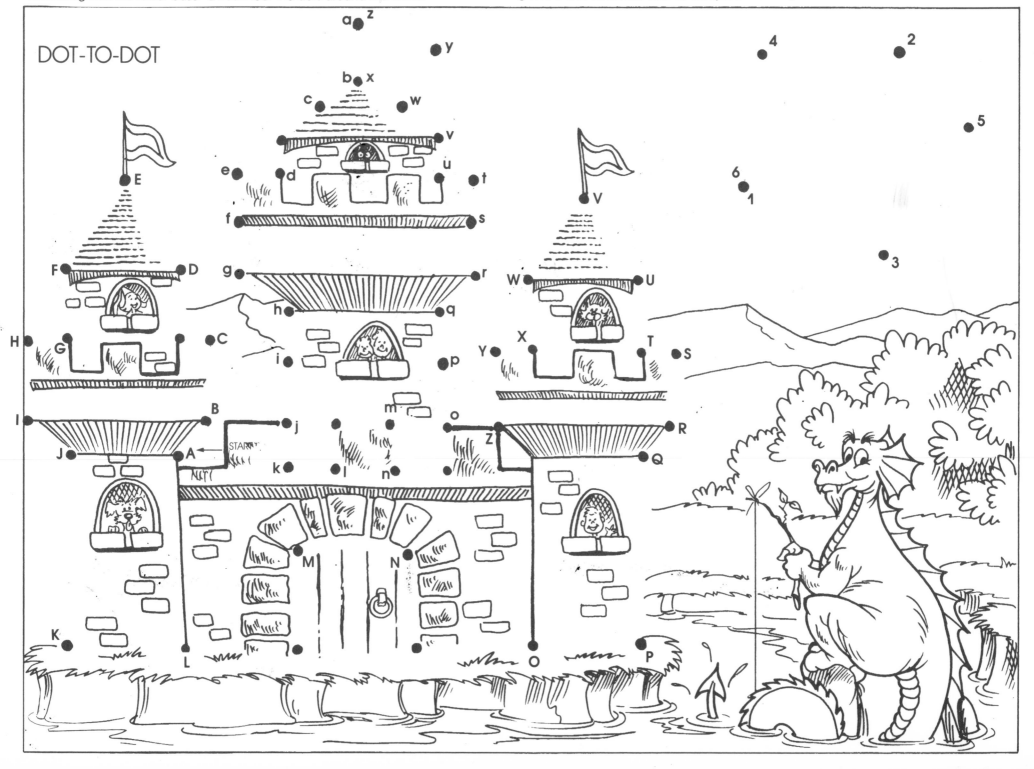

DOT-TO-DOT

1. Starting with the capital "A", connect the dots around the castle.
2. Starting with the lower case "a". connect the dots around the tower.
3. Starting with #1, connect the dots to complete the shape.

Aa Bb Cc Dd Ee Ff Gg Hh Ii Jj Kk Ll Mm Nn Oo Pp Qq Rr Ss Tt Uu Vv Ww Xx Yy Zz

Trace the letters. Fill in the missing letters.

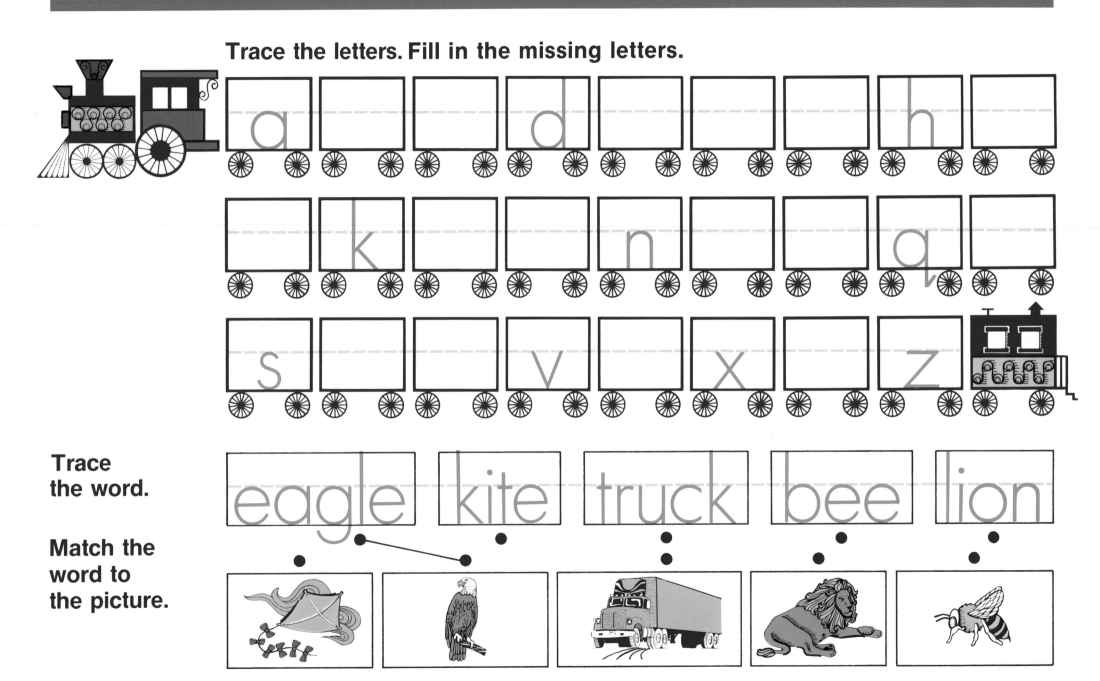

Trace the word.

eagle kite truck bee lion

Match the word to the picture.

Aa Bb Cc Dd Ee Ff Gg Hh Ii Jj Kk Ll Mm Nn Oo Pp Qq Rr Ss Tt Uu Vv Ww Xx Yy Zz

To practice here, turn the book around and flip the plastic page.

Learning to write words.

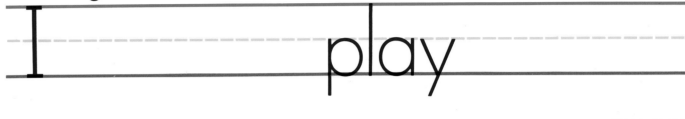

I   play

with   toys

TO PARENT AND TEACHER:

Directions for your child:
1. Trace the word with a finger.
2. Trace the word with the pencil.
3. Write the word in the empty space.

Directions for your child:
1. Trace the sentence with a finger.
2. Trace the sentence with the pencil.
3. Write the sentence in the empty space.
4. Leave space between words.

Learning to write a sentence.

I play with toys.

I play with toys.

AaBbCcDdEeFfGgHhIiJjKkLlMmNnOoPpQqRrSsTtUuVvWwXxYyZz

To practice here, turn the book around and flip the plastic page.